EXPRESS YOUR LIGHT

SPIRITUAL TRUTHS FOR EVERYDAY LIFE

ERIC JOHN CAMPBELL

GROUNDED GROVE
PUBLISHING

EXPRESS YOUR LIGHT

CONTENTS

1. Your Light Is Powerful   1
2. Your True Nature Is Play   9
3. How To Change Your Beliefs   15
4. Surrender Your Ego   23
5. Return To Your Natural State   35
6. You're A Channel For Love   45

About The Author   53
Stay Connected With The Author   55

1

YOUR LIGHT IS POWERFUL

THIS BOOK IS FOR EVERYBODY WHO WISHES TO LIVE A happier, more fulfilling life. The Universe desires this for everyone and has made your world a playground for you to experiment, play, and create in.

The Universe wants you to create beautiful things so it can experience them. It's through you and your human body that the Universe can experience itself.

The planet you're living in is indeed your world. It's the kingdom you inherited as soon as you were born, and since you're a divine child of the Universe, you must realize how loved you are.

The Universe has an endless stream of unconditional love for you and looks at you with this love through all the things you consider shameful and evil. There is nothing you can do that would stop the Universe from loving you.

Before we go any further, we must address a question you may have: *how could the Universe make life so cruel for many of its children whom it loves?*

As a parent, you want your child to feel free so they don't need you to do everything. In the same way, the Universe would like to intervene as little as possible so that you may figure it out on your own. The more you can do this, the greater your ability to use the power of creative thought to make things that have never existed before.

You must realize that the Universe loves every single bit of you and all you've done. In the eyes of the Universe, you're perfect exactly as you are now and always will be, no matter what you do in the future. You're a deeply loved Soul, and the Universe wants nothing more than to see your light shine.

Within everyone is pure light. This light is the Universe's infinite, unconditional love. The Universe wants you to use this light to create beautiful things in your world, which is how you'll bring heaven to earth.

Have you ever been so touched by a work of art that it moved you to tears? Has a piece of music ever given you a tingling sensation throughout your body? These feelings are what happens when someone else's light touches you. Light is powerful.

The beautiful thing about this light is that every single human has it. The light of the Universe lives in you. Having this light means you're always connected to the Universe's unconditional love and have nothing to fear.

A problem only arises when you hide your light. Contrary to what many people believe, no dark or evil forces can stop you from shining your light. You're the only one who decides whether or not you share your light with the world.

By observing others, you may have learned that your light is dangerous, will cause you to be unloved, or isn't worth sharing. Not expressing your light is painful because your whole purpose in being born on earth is to shine it fully.

When you hide your light, you experience the fear of feeling unloved. Fear comes from the absence of light. Everyone needs light to survive and especially to thrive. Light is unconditional love from the Universe and is more important than food or water.

If people don't connect to the light within themselves, they may do horrible things to others in an attempt to feel love. It's tough to watch people do this to each other, but the Universe looks at everyone with pure love. The Universe doesn't love one person more or less than another, which is why its love for you is unconditional.

The people that are doing the most horrific things need love the most. These people need you to send them light so they may see how loved they are. When these people experience how deep the Universe's love for them is, they'll stop doing these horrible things.

The Universe wants you to express your light more. Shining your light is the best way to heal your world. When you shine your light, you become a sun radiating love for all others to enjoy.

Light and love are two words that point to the same energy. The beautiful thing about this energy is that an infinite well of it lives within every individual.

The Universe has unlimited love to give you and wants nothing more than for you to express it. You can best express this light through your creative acts. You were born to create in this world, and it's how you bring heaven to earth.

You become a channel for the Universe's love whenever you create something. It doesn't matter what you make. You can share the Universe's love through a meal, poem, song, dance, or anything else you can imagine.

The amount of light you express has nothing to do with how famous or beautiful your creations are. The Universe doesn't see art as good or bad and instead sees all created things with the same unconditional love it has for you. *How could the Universe not love its child's creations?* Every time you shine your light, you bring more of the Universe's love into your world.

There is never a wrong way to share the Universe's love through your creations. The Universe's wish for you is that you don't let any judgments stop you from creating. You're a divine child of the Universe and an endless sea of light lives within you.

You need to express this light living inside you. You're cutting yourself off from the Universe's love when you don't share your light. Without this love, life can seem unkind even though all the love is already inside you, waiting to come out.

The most important thing to know about the Universe's love is that you must express it to feel it. You can have many loving thoughts and feelings, but that love only takes proper form once you share it.

By being a vessel for the Universe's love, you're most able to feel it, which is why you hear so many people talk about how great it feels to give.

One of the most dominant beliefs that stop people from sharing their light is believing they must be practical to survive. You'll experience feelings of heaviness and fatigue anytime you sacrifice your creative expression to be practical.

Shining your light is the most natural thing for your body. To not express your light requires effort, and this effort is what you often call being practical.

There is always an opportunity to express the Universe's love. You can add this love to the breakfast you cook in the morning or how you treat your body while brushing your teeth. You don't need to quit everything and become a full-time artist to express and feel the Universe's love.

Using the need to be practical as an excuse for hiding your light is a way of protecting yourself from fear. Believing that you need more money, time, or energy is an illusion. It may feel like you need more of these things before you can share your light with the world, but you don't.

So why do people hide their light? It's different for each person, but usually, it's because of its power. When you express your light, you draw other people to you. If you grew up surrounded by darker energies, you likely learned to hide your light to avoid attracting unwanted attention.

The light living within you is something you can never lose. It was there with you the moment you were born and will be with you when you leave this life. This light is your real personality.

Most of your personality up until now are unconscious patterns you've learned over time. These patterns aren't the real you. As you begin expressing more of your light, you'll get to know your true self, which is the self that channels the Universe's love.

When you begin expressing your light regularly, you'll discover how light channels through you differs from how light channels through others. The unique way light shines through you is your authentic personality.

It's so much fun to be your true self! You never need to fear giving up the false self your upbringing has conditioned you to believe you are. This false self isn't the real you, and as soon as you let it go, you'll see how wonderful this life the Universe has created for you is.

For this book's sake, we'll call that false, conditioned self the ego. The ego isn't something you're born with. It also isn't this scary, mysterious thing that continually gets in the way of your joy. Your ego is the sum of all your conditioned responses that stop you from shining your light. The longer you hide your light, the stronger your ego becomes.

The beautiful thing about your ego is that you can quickly let it go if you choose to. You can give up your ego and immediately start living from your light. The idea that getting rid of your ego is a long, drawn-out process is a limiting belief that you can easily change.

The best way to live from your light is to focus on the positives rather than trying to fix the negatives. When you truly focus on the positives, the negatives have a way of resolving themselves. These seemingly negative things are illusions and outward manifestations of the fear that gives your ego its power.

2

YOUR TRUE NATURE IS PLAY

YOUR MOST NATURAL STATE IS TO EXIST AS PURE LIGHT. You're born to be happy, life is supposed to work, and the Universe created your world as a playground for you to enjoy. You're here to make things in this world and to enjoy the creative process.

Your fear of spending most of your life doing work you dislike exists because it goes directly against your true nature, which is play. You're born to build things with childlike wonder, and this book aims to get you back to your natural state.

By embodying this feeling of play, you'll feel at home here on earth and see why it's a beautiful kingdom you've inherited. The Universe made this world for you and wants nothing more than to see you create with pure joy.

The next topic we must talk about is money. This topic carries a lot of weight for many people because they believe it is why they can no longer live from their light.

Before money came into your life, you were a carefree kid who played with the beauty of the Universe's love channeling through you. As a kid, you effortlessly created beautiful things overflowing with unconditional love. But then it became time to grow up, enter the real world, and become an adult.

The hardest part for the Universe to watch in anyone's life is the day they start refusing to play. This day is when you begin exerting effort to stop yourself from expressing your most natural state. In a way, it's the day many die before their time.

From that moment on, you're no longer living from your light. When the light shuts off, the ego starts to grow. The ego can become very powerful if you go too long without sharing your light. The most important thing for you to know about your light is that you'll have no better feeling than expressing it.

Your world's pleasures are enjoyable, but they're not nearly as satisfying as the feeling you get when fully shining your light. By shining your light, you'll feel free, knowing you're where you're supposed to be, doing what you're born to do.

A skeptical part of you likely doesn't believe these words and thinks this is all wishful thinking. This part of you is your conditioned ego, and it's saying this because it has gathered evidence that your world doesn't work this way.

The vital thing you must realize about life on earth is that your beliefs create your reality. When you believe something is true, you begin noticing and attracting things in your world that confirm your belief.

For example, if you believe it's impossible to express your light and the world you live in is set up so that you must suffer to survive, you'll gather evidence that supports this belief.

If you have this belief, you'll surround yourself with people who work on things they don't enjoy, thinking it's necessary. You'll also find yourself watching movies and reading news articles that further reinforce your belief.

Your beliefs are a magnet. What you believe to be true starts a magnetic pull, and the stronger your belief is, the more evidence you'll attract that supports it.

Having your beliefs be a magnet is a beautiful design of your world. It means you can hold any belief in your mind, and with enough faith, you'll attract that life to you.

Everybody has faith. Many people believe that faith is something they need to work on that requires lots of practice and daily mantras, but everyone already has faith in something.

Whatever world you're living in now exists because of your faith in your beliefs. At some point on your journey, the beliefs came that attracted every life circumstance you're experiencing now. If you had faith that you must work hard to survive, this belief started a magnetic pull that attracted that life to you.

When you're a kid becoming an adult, you tend to inherit the beliefs your parents and society believe in. Inheriting beliefs is part of the beautiful design of your world.

When future parents and most of society believe that life is fun and everyone is born to express their light, the children will naturally inherit this belief. When the most popular beliefs in your world come from love, everyone born on earth will intuitively know how to live their fullest potential.

At this moment, the most dominant belief in your society is that life isn't supposed to be easy. This belief says struggling and sacrifice are required to live a happy life. Since this has been the most dominant belief for a long time, most people you've grown up with inherited it and see it as truth because their parents and the society they grew up in believed it.

As long as you don't consciously decide to change your beliefs, you'll keep getting the same results. It's life-changing to learn how to change your beliefs. It doesn't matter how hard you've worked, how long you've put in your dues, or how good a person you've been. By the design of your world, you can only receive the happiness you're looking for once your beliefs match this desire.

To live the life your heart dreams of, you must become aware of the beliefs you've picked up. You can only do something to change your beliefs once you identify them and recognize the power they have in your life. Naming your beliefs starts the process of taking your power back.

No matter what state your life is in now, it's not this way because of anything outside yourself. You're not a victim of parents that emotionally scarred you, a heartless ex-lover, an evil boss, or a broken society.

Everything in your life now is there because you inherited particular beliefs and put enough faith in them to magnetize your present life circumstances. Hopefully, this begins to empower you. There is no need to judge yourself for having done this.

The Universe loves you unconditionally and wants you to adopt new beliefs that align with your heart. Changing your beliefs is the secret to manifesting your unique version of heaven on earth.

3

HOW TO CHANGE YOUR BELIEFS

CHANGING ANY OF YOUR BELIEFS IS EASY. ALL YOU must do is choose the belief you want to change, write out a new belief you want to replace it with and gather evidence that supports your new belief.

The hardest part about this process isn't identifying your current belief, choosing a new belief, or gathering evidence that supports your new belief. You can do all these things quickly with little effort.

The most challenging thing you'll have to do is dismiss any evidence that seems to fuel your old belief. As long as the conversations you're in and the books you read reinforce your old belief, you won't believe your new belief is true.

You can see this most easily in your relationship

with money. Many people believe money is challenging to make, and they must work hard on things they don't want to do to survive.

For this example, we're not saying this belief is good or bad, but if you want a different life, you may have to change it. Let us assume the new belief you want to live from is that money flows to you abundantly when you pursue your passions.

Notice how your body feels when you read this new belief. *Is your mind already having thoughts saying this is wishful thinking? Do you feel anger or discomfort and don't know why?* We won't do anything with these thoughts and emotions, but bringing awareness to what comes up within you is essential.

All we've done so far is state an old belief and suggest a new one. Next, we must dismiss any evidence that supports your old belief. To do this, you must become aware of the information you take in daily.

For example, if your friend complains about receiving a parking ticket they can't afford, it could reinforce your old belief. A movie about someone struggling to make a living could also reinforce it. There are lots of ways in which you may gather evidence that supports your old belief.

If you've lived with a particular belief for a long

time, you'll likely be surprised at how much evidence you've attracted into your life that supports it. It may seem like every person on earth is struggling to make money, and all movies are about someone who works tirelessly to make a living. If you feel this way, you've held this belief for a long time and have magnetized lots of evidence that supports it.

The amount of evidence you see when you become consciously aware of a belief can be overwhelming. Suddenly, you may feel that every conversation you participate in and any video you watch supports your old belief.

Feeling this way is an excellent thing. It may feel like you're overwhelmed, and finding new evidence is near impossible, but you would only see things this way if you were becoming aware of why your old belief felt so real.

With awareness comes the ability to make a different choice. By fully understanding how your beliefs work, the world becomes your playground. You're not the victim of a cruel world you were born into by accident and instead have inherited a glorious kingdom where the beliefs you put your faith into create your reality.

Earth is a beautiful sandbox with infinite creative

potential. You'll feel motivated to change your beliefs when you realize you can manifest any life your heart desires.

You must hold onto your new beliefs even if the evidence you attract in your daily life seems to disprove them. With time you'll draw enough evidence to your new beliefs that they become more powerful than your old ones.

The hardest part about integrating a new belief is becoming mindful of your conversations—both the conversations you're having with yourself and those you're having with other people.

To change the subject with one of your loved ones takes courage. It's tough to tell someone you're close with that you can no longer discuss specific topics with them. It may feel like you're abandoning your friend or saying the way a loved one of yours is choosing to live their life is wrong, but it's for the highest good of all that you do this.

Changing your beliefs to align with your heart is the most important thing you can do for yourself and your world. By adopting these new beliefs, you'll find the Universe abundantly supporting you in all areas of your life.

Living with heart-centered beliefs makes you feel significantly happier and more alive. There are no limits on how good your life can get. Every day has the potential to overwhelm you with its beauty.

By shining your light as brightly as possible, you inspire everyone you cross paths with to do the same. You have the power to start a chain reaction where your light helps ignite the light of millions. When enough people fully shine their light, that will become the default belief the next generation inherits.

You must not talk about or consume any information that reinforces your old beliefs, even if it's painful for a person you love and you feel you're abandoning them.

Setting this boundary is for the highest good of all, including your loved ones. For example, suppose you refuse to participate in or listen to conversations reinforcing the belief that money is hard to make.

By doing this, you're a leader creating a boundary that sets an example for others. Proactively changing your beliefs has a ripple effect that powerfully impacts your world in ways your mind can't see.

Up until this point, we've used money as our example. I've chosen this example because most people can relate to it, and it's easy to see how your life circumstances reflect your beliefs about money.

Everything we've discussed so far also applies to any other beliefs you may have. If your heart desires something and you feel you can't have it, a limiting belief is getting in the way.

The next area of life we'll focus on is romantic relationships. Look for your inherited beliefs if you have trouble finding a romantic partner. *What was modeled for you by your parents and society?* The beliefs you witnessed growing up are likely the ones you've taken on and live from today.

At this stage, it's easy to place blame and become a victim. It's easy to say your parents or society never showed you how to have a healthy romantic relationship. *Can you see how these thoughts reinforce your limiting beliefs?* They can strengthen the idea that romantic relationships are challenging because of the programming you learned as a child.

You can change these limiting beliefs in an instant. If you want to make this change, you have to decide not to be a victim. By making this choice, you're letting go of your victim story and inheriting your power as a divine child of the Universe.

You can change any of your beliefs right now. There is no length of time required to do this. Your world can become a hundred times better in an instant by adopting heart-centered beliefs. You hold all the power. You can bring heaven to earth right now.

It doesn't matter whether you change your beliefs about money, romantic relationships, or something else. You can change any belief. Once you consciously change one of them, you'll realize you can change any of them. You can manifest all your heart's desires, and the Universe wants nothing more than for you to create a life you love.

It's important to note that you can change any belief on your own without needing the support of another person. It might be helpful for you to collaborate with a loved one when changing one of your beliefs, but it's not necessary.

Thinking you need permission or the right life circumstances to align before you can change your beliefs is the biggest roadblock you'll encounter. You're ready now, and you already have everything you need.

Once you start living from your new beliefs, life will look entirely different to you than it did before. Life will look different because you'll fundamentally change how you see the world. You'll go from being a victim to becoming a master of your fate.

As you become a more conscious creator of your life, you may wonder whether you have free will or if everything in your life is predetermined. This question bothers many people, and it can feel like you need to know the answer to be happy.

Knowing the answer to this question isn't necessary. If it's fun to think about, go for it, but if it's making your body feel heavy, let it go. All you need to know is that you must feel the answer to this question.

Nobody can answer this question with words. It's neither. Your ego doesn't have as much free will as it believes it has, and your life isn't predetermined. There are limitless potential life paths you may choose to walk that are constantly changing.

The only thing you need to know about this topic is that you'll never be satisfied as long as your ego is in the driver's seat of your life. Your ego is a collection of conditioned responses you've learned over time that doesn't know what is best for you.

As long as your ego is driving, your life will never change. It can't change when you're responding to your life circumstances in the same way you have before, which is why you must surrender your ego.

4

SURRENDER YOUR EGO

YOUR INTUITION IS THE PART OF YOURSELF YOU WANT in the driver's seat of your life. Intuition is called many things, such as a gut feeling, your heart, or channeling your higher self. It doesn't matter what you name it, but it does matter that you follow it.

The best way to follow your intuition is to prioritize your body's feelings. If your body feels light and relaxed, you're in alignment. If your body feels tense and anxious, you're out of alignment.

The Universe created your world to be a playground for you to enjoy. An essential part of that design is giving you a body that alerts you when you're out of alignment and makes you feel wonderful when you're in alignment.

One thing that will come up when you start

living from your intuition is fear. Putting yourself into alignment will cause you to do things that make no sense to your ego. It will seem like many of your actions threaten your safety because they go against what your ego has learned to survive.

Trusting your intuition is the painful part of coming into alignment that stops many people from manifesting a life they love. What will help you as you make this transition is to not seek approval outside of yourself. Have faith in the Universe and yourself.

As you begin this process, the deeper part of you will feel a sense of peace. This deeper part of you will be grateful that you're coming into alignment and back home to who you truly are. Your ego, on the other hand, will become very scared. One thing it will do when it's worried is look for approval from people outside yourself.

You'll suddenly feel the urge to share what you're doing to live from your heart with your friends and loved ones. By doing this, your ego is looking for others to confirm that you're doing the right thing so it feels safe.

Looking for validation isn't a problem if you've surrounded yourself with people living from their hearts. These people will understand that what your heart guides you to do often makes no sense to your mind. But if you've been living from your ego's conditioned responses, you won't be surrounded by people like this.

When you go to the people in your life now seeking approval for the actions your heart is guiding you to do, they'll likely reflect the same thoughts that your ego tells you. These thoughts may include: you're *crazy, what you're doing makes no sense, stick to what you know to be safe, and this isn't how your world works.*

You must give yourself the validation that you're doing the right thing by following your heart. This validation can't come from your ego or someone outside yourself and instead can only come from the deeper part of you that knows.

Meditation is a way to get in touch with this deeper part of yourself, but it's not the only way. Anything that makes you feel light and like a little kid helps, such as being in nature, singing, dancing, playing, and acting.

At first, it will be hard to distinguish between actions coming from your ego and your heart. Just like learning anything new, you'll make more mistakes initially. You may do something you think is coming from your heart, but it doesn't feel right after you start doing it.

How your body feels is the best indicator to determine whether your actions come from your heart or mind. If you start doing something and your body feels heavy, tired, and resistant, then stop doing that thing.

You know you're living from your heart if your body feels light, playful, and at ease. The beautiful thing about this is the more you practice living this way, the better you'll get at it.

Living from your heart is your most natural state of being. You're born to live this way, and by doing so, you become a beacon of light inspiring others to do the same.

Life is supposed to be easy, and if you feel good while doing something, that is because it's for your highest good to do it. If you don't feel good while doing something, the Universe is guiding you to do something else instead.

Now we must talk about surrender. Your ego may believe this sounds great, but you need to be practical and make money to survive in the real world. Remember, your ego is just a sum of all the conditioned responses you've learned over time, mostly inherited from your parents and society.

Your ego's beliefs only feel real because you've put your faith in them for years and have attracted lots of evidence that reinforces them. The belief that you must do things you don't enjoy to survive can be changed easily, but if you're living from that belief, following your heart can feel like madness. It can feel like you're a crazy person in your society and irresponsible.

To stop these feelings from getting stronger, you must seek approval from yourself and not from others outside of you. To help you find this approval within yourself, I will explain why following your heart is so powerful.

Your ego is the sum of the conditioned responses you've learned from past experiences and therefore makes decisions with very little data. But your heart, intuition, whatever you want to call this place of knowing within you, is connected to all that exists.

Your heart is one with the entire Universe connecting you with all humans, animals, and plants on earth. Your heart knows what is best for you and all living beings, which is why following it is essential.

The actions your heart guides you to do often make no sense to your ego because of its limited perspective. Your ego sees your world from the single worldview created by your past experiences and beliefs, but your heart connects to all of existence.

Instead of thinking of your world as a rock with trillions of separate living organisms, see it as one living being. You're not an independent, autonomous organism. You're one with the entire Universe, and its infinite intelligence is constantly manifesting itself through your intuition. The heart you're listening to is the whole organism guiding you on the best thing you can do.

You'll feel terrific when you align entirely with the one living being. By surrendering your ego and living from your heart, you'll find yourself effortlessly taking aligned actions while feeling a deep connection to your planet and everything in it. You become a living expression of the Universe's infinite love when you follow your heart.

When you're in alignment, you'll find the Universe abundantly supporting you in wealth, love, and joy. The Universe created your life to be fun and flow with great ease.

The hardest part about becoming one with the Universe is letting go of your ideas of how your world works. You don't know how the world you live in works. You may think you know, but that is only a belief. By the Universe's design, you can't understand the world you live in through your thinking mind.

When most people hear this, they feel fear of the unknown. *It may feel like the beliefs you used to stand on don't exist anymore, but why is this so scary? Why is it so frightening that you don't know how your world works?*

You don't know how your body works. There are trillions of chemical reactions and actions happening every moment. *Does this scare you? Do you see how trying to understand every detail of how your body works is pointless?*

It sounds strange that anyone would do this, but trying to understand how your world works is no different. Just like trillions of actions constantly happen inside your body, trillions also occur outside your body.

You can never fully understand why things in your life are the way they are. You can never know why someone responds in the way that they do to a specific statement you make, how your next sum of money will enter your life, how the flowers outside your house grow, and why your new boss is rewarding someone else even though you've worked harder than them.

Trying to understand why everything in your life is the way it is will drive you crazy. The Universe didn't design your mind to understand everything. If you believe you control your life, that is an illusion.

You're not in control. You don't know what tomorrow will bring. But just because you don't understand these things doesn't mean you're in danger. It doesn't mean you'll be the victim of something you don't understand.

The Universe loves you unconditionally and created a world to support and nurture you. An issue only arises when your ego tries to take the driver's seat and starts believing your world is hostile.

If you believe your world is unsafe and you're only surviving because of things you're in control of, your anxiety will be endless. If anyone threatens this idea that you're in control, it will scare you tremendously if you believe that control is the only thing keeping you safe.

What I'm offering you now is permission to let go. Let go, even though it feels scary. Let go even though your mind is yelling at you to do otherwise. Let go and surrender to the flow of life.

When you let go, you'll experience peace and joy. You'll realize you were never in control and the Universe always supported you. The more you live with this faith, the more open you'll be to beautiful new things entering your life.

Since you're not in control, you may wonder what you have power over. *Doesn't this mean it's all predetermined?* The truth is, no. You do have a choice, and it's a simple one. The choice is: *do you live from faith or fear?*

In every moment, you intuitively know what to do. Your body shows you what to do by how it feels. Your body naturally wants to take actions that make you feel light and free. This process happens entirely on its own. If you didn't try to control your life, you would automatically stop doing things that make you feel bad and only do things that make you feel good.

Therefore your choice in every moment is: *do you have faith to do what your body's feelings guide you to do?* If nothing feels light and everything feels heavy, then you can do nothing. Eventually, an action that feels light and exciting will come up. It always does. When that light action arises, you can go for it with complete faith that you're supported or resist it and do something that feels heavier out of fear.

Your most natural state of being is to choose to do the things that feel light and easy. Not living this way requires tremendous force and energy, which is why you can hardly do anything and feel so tired. If what you're doing isn't in alignment, your body will give you lots of physical symptoms to try and get you back into alignment.

You exercise your faith in the Universe when you take the lightest feeling actions. An action feels light and easy because doing it is for your highest good. These intuitive actions may seem pointless or impractical to your ego but remember, your ego only sees a limited perspective of all that exists.

By having faith in what you can't see, you're surrendering the illusion of control, and that is when you truly live. You'll experience heaven on earth by letting go, and all your heart's deepest dreams will come true.

Keep taking the lightest actions with complete faith that they're for your highest good. Consistently choosing the lightest feeling actions is the only lesson you must embody to live an overwhelmingly happy and abundant life. So much joy is waiting for you right now, and all you have to do to receive it is choose faith over fear consistently.

At first, this will take a lot of effort to do. It will seem like you're crazy, and terrible things are coming. But if you consistently choose the lightest feeling actions, you'll find that your life doesn't fall apart, and a seemingly magical set of circumstances take care of you. After reaching this point, it becomes effortless to follow the lightest actions.

When your faith is unconditional, you'll automatically choose the lightest actions with great excitement. You'll love not knowing what beautiful things will enter your life and support you next. Living this way is so much fun!

Trusting the Universe is much better than always knowing what is coming next, which is all your mind wants; guaranteed safety. If your life were predetermined, it would be boring because you would know what was coming before it came.

On the other hand, life will seem magical when you live every day with the faith you're supported, but you have no idea how that support will come. Living this way brings you into the present and shows that every moment is a blessing and an adventure. Living from your heart is the ultimate truth, filling every part of your being with peace, love, and joy.

Your society raised you to do things with effort through school and work, but the problem with effort is it's usually unnatural. Sometimes, you'll need to use effort, but it's not your natural way of being.

To live a life of truth requires no effort. You don't need to exert effort to create art, manifest money, or have great relationships. As long as you're in alignment with your heart, these things happen on their own. The feeling of effort is only required if you want to return to your natural state.

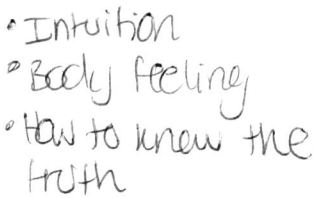

- Intuition
- Body feeling
- How to know the truth

5

RETURN TO YOUR NATURAL STATE

Your most natural state is to go through your day, taking the lightest feeling actions. To not live this way requires effort. Going to a job you dislike every day takes effort. If you have been exerting this effort every day for years, you likely have the belief that you must exert lots of effort to survive. *But do kids need to use effort to play?*

Returning to your most natural state is a blissful experience because the need for effort falls away. Instead of feeling like you have to force things, you let things unfold organically. A life in alignment is one where you're excited to get up in the morning. It's a life lived from inspiration rather than discipline.

Exerting effort can be helpful if used

intentionally. It can get you to let go of learned behavior that no longer serves you. If you have been choosing heavy actions for years, selecting the lightest feeling actions will take a lot of effort.

You create an unconscious cycle that reinforces your beliefs whenever you form a habit. Breaking free from this cycle requires effort. To do something that goes against your current beliefs about how your world works takes willpower. Know that you won't always need this discipline.

Your most natural state is to live as carefree as a child, where effort and discipline aren't required. The belief that makes you believe effort and discipline are necessary to live a happy life limits your freedom. You're born to flow through your day, taking only the lightest feeling actions. By light, I mean the actions that feel most exciting and easy.

Right now, as you read this book, I hope this is the lightest action for you. If reading this book makes you feel heavy, put it down. You never need to take actions that feel heavy, even if you believe they'll help you be happier in the future.

The next topic we must discuss is you are your greatest teacher. No one outside of you knows what is best for you. Even this book is helpful only because of how you look at it, which is why you must stay connected to the feelings in your body as you live your life.

Instead of looking for truth in words, pay attention to your feelings. Let go of using your mind to discern whether someone's words contain truth and listen to your body. While listening to the words of others, notice if your heart feels tight or loose, the tension in your jaw, and how your gut responds. These are all indicators for you to follow.

Although you may come across some sources of information that contain more truth than others, it never means to worship it. Nothing outside of yourself can ever be a reliable source of truth. All the wisdom you ever need lives inside your body.

Even though there are universal truths, people are at different stages in their growth. Therefore a life-changing book or video your loved one recommends may not be a good fit for you.

Plenty of sources contain truth because each reveals the truth already living inside you. Trust yourself and the way your body feels when you hear something. Information that makes your body feel lighter and more free contains truth. It doesn't matter if you're watching a television show, a commercial, or reading a gossipy magazine. Pay attention to how your body feels and let go of appearances.

You've probably heard from many people to avoid the news or limit your consumption, but this isn't always good advice. Taking this action out of effort and discipline will bring you feelings of heaviness.

You must only stop looking at the news if doing so makes your body feel heavier and tighter. *Can you see how much difference you'll feel if you make decisions based on your body's feelings instead of relying on your mind?* Both paths achieve the same outcome of not watching the news, but one requires constant discipline while the other is effortless.

The actions that you take in your life aren't important. What matters is where you're coming from when participating in those actions. You could be a vegan who meditates for two hours daily and compliments your loved ones often because that is the best advice you've heard to be happy and still be dissatisfied with your life.

If you force yourself to do things that make your body feel heavy, they'll never bring you joy. You could also be doing all these same things and happy. The difference is where you're coming from. If it feels light and easy, keep doing it!

There could also be someone who eats unhealthy foods and watches TV shows all day, living a heart-centered life. If this person feels light and free while doing these activities, they're in alignment.

A big concern for many is that they'll do lazy and unproductive activities all day after giving up control. The fear is that your effort keeps your life together, but your life will fall apart without it.

You may have had some days when you were sick and did nothing productive when you had time off work. Living an entire life with this much freedom may sound terrifying. What you must remember is why specific actions feel light and easy.

Life is supposed to feel effortless. You're born to keep choosing the lightest feeling actions and be supported abundantly as you do this. If an action feels light, it's because doing it serves your highest good.

When you stop choosing heavier actions and have more free time, your body will initially want to unwind. Your body needs rest if you've been exerting effort for many years.

By doing these activities that seem lazy and unproductive, your body is returning to its most natural state. Doing nothing for a few days or weeks may be the best action for your highest good. If that is the lightest action for you to take, then it's in alignment.

Your mind's fear will try to keep you safe, so it will get scared when it feels like you're doing nothing productive for a long time. If you've been watching TV shows for a week straight, it may bring up scary thoughts such as *you can't live like this for the rest of your life, and what you're doing is unsustainable, which is why you need discipline.*

But the fear that comes from your ego has a limited perspective. Your ego can't see that your actions now may raise your vibration and prepare you to birth beautiful creative gifts into your world.

Fear from your mind only sees what is happening now and projects your present onto your future. Your mind also searches your past for evidence supporting your fears. The solution isn't to fight your mind or to make it wrong. The answer is to stop identifying with your mind and instead live from your heart.

Fear is an illusion. Fear isn't real. Your worst fears will never come true, no matter what happens. If you fear losing your job, you'll only lose it if it's in your highest good to do so.

Your deepest fears will never come true because

they're usually not about what appearances suggest. For example, you may think you fear losing your job, but the real fear is believing you'll lose everything you own and can't provide for the people you love.

You may lose your job when you jump into alignment, but you still won't realize your underlying fear. Even though your deeper fears will never come true, most people don't let themselves make it to that point.

Most people don't follow their intuition because they believe their fear is real. But fear is never real. Fear is always an illusion. Your ego projects its fears onto the world, but you can sail through them unharmed if you keep your faith.

Imagine sailing a boat and seeing an ominous thick gray cloud ahead of you. The closer you get to this cloud, the more frightening it seems until you're face-to-face with it. When you're about to sail into this cloud, it feels like your entire life is falling apart.

Most people turn their boats around at this point. But if you keep sailing, you'll see that your boat cuts through the cloud. The cloud is an illusion, and you can sail through unharmed.

On the other side of this cloud is an oasis waiting for you. It's the living experience of heaven on earth. But to get there, you must keep sailing without turning around. Fear feels real up until you rub shoulders with it. As soon as you try to touch your fear, you'll realize it doesn't exist.

Even if you lose your job and do nothing productive because that is the lightest action for you, somehow things will work out. They always do. Keep taking the lightest actions, and you'll see that the fears that come up along the way are illusions.

You'll witness the fear in your mind and know the truth in your heart. The more you pay attention to how your entire body feels, the safer and more protected you'll feel.

It's possible to be in the center of that ominous gray cloud feeling like your life is falling apart in every way, and still be at peace. When you see your life circumstances through your heart's eyes rather than the eyes of your mind, you'll find inner peace, which is unshakeable.

Once you find this peace within yourself, it can never be forgotten or lost. This peace is waiting for you, and the quickest way to get there is by paying close attention to how your body feels while you continue choosing the lightest actions.

As you do this, your mind will come up with many reasons why everything we've discussed so far isn't true. You may know someone who seems to exert no effort, watches TV shows constantly, and appears unhappy.

What is important to remember is not to be fooled by appearances. Earlier, we discussed how someone might be aligned or not based on how their heart feels while participating in an activity. Watching a lot of TV shows might not be the lightest action for you, or it may be the lightest action, and then after a couple of days, the idea of watching more TV shows feels heavy.

There is a natural rhythm to life that you must learn to trust. Every day is a new day, and the actions your body feels like doing today have nothing to do with the actions you chose yesterday. You'll never get lost if you stay connected to how your body and heart feel.

When you keep choosing the lightest actions, your life becomes magical. You begin feeling the Universe supporting you in ways your ego can't understand. The more you live this way, the lighter your body feels.

Soon you'll choose the lightest action in each moment by default without any effort. From this place, you experience the carefree joy and freedom of a child but with the awareness and abilities of an adult.

What we've talked about for most of this book is how to return to your most natural state by changing your beliefs and choosing the lightest actions. *But what happens once you permanently live in your most natural state?*

✳ The answer is the Universe's love enters your world through you. By living in your most natural state, the Universe uses you as a channel to birth art into your world, which is how all masterpieces are born.

6

YOU'RE A CHANNEL FOR LOVE

YOU COLLABORATE WITH A POWERFUL FORCE WHEN the Universe's love channels through you. Because you're the channel, the way this love flows through you is unique. Your self-expression becomes the direct expression of the Universe's unconditional love.

Remember how I mentioned that the Universe has the same unconditional love for you as everyone else? The Universe is only able to express that love through you.

When you create things, you bring more of the Universe's love into your world. Creating is what you're born to do. Every time you create something, you'll feel deep joy within your heart.

You allow the Universe's love to live through you

and experience your world when you create. As the energy of the Universe flows through you, your body feels the sensation of unconditional love. As you continue choosing the lightest actions, your ego fades, and you become a more pure channel for the Universe's love to flow through.

There are no limits to the amount of love you can feel and how beautiful your life can become. Any limits that get in the way are just beliefs picked up by your ego. You have the power to change any belief. The more you let your limiting beliefs go and align yourself with your heart, the happier you'll become.

Your life can feel like magic. You're born to birth beautiful things into your world, and the time to do so is now. Everything you've been learning in this book is to help you return to your most natural state and be a channel for the Universe's love, which is your purpose for being here on earth. When others experience this love, they feel lighter and are likelier to become a channel for it themselves.

As you express more of the Universe's love, you birth incredible things into your world. Through this collaborative act, you create things that the Universe could never make without you, which is why earth is your playground.

Your world is a creative space where you can create anything your heart desires. Your creative acts are pioneering because they bring things into your world that never existed before. Creating is so much fun! Everything you create while living from your heart radiates unconditional love.

Have you ever wondered why some creations attract attention while others don't? The more you create something with love, the more people you attract to it. When other people experience what you make, they feel the Universe's love for them, which is the love you brought into your world.

When people feel the Universe's love while experiencing your creations, you grow the love inside yourself. This love makes you feel lighter and able to channel more of the Universe's love through you.

The love you express through your creative acts is the same love others express through their creative acts. The only difference is the manifestation you choose for this love, which is why experiencing art in many forms is nourishing.

Art is a way for you to feel love. The less someone expresses their light, the more likely they'll be to consume and enjoy the art channeled by others. If someone isn't connected to and expressing the light within themself, they'll look for it elsewhere.

Looking outside oneself for love leads many people to consume the art created by others compulsively. There is nothing wrong with watching TV shows or movies, but if doing so is your only source of love, you'll feel something is missing. Enjoying the art others have channeled is beautiful and will fill you with love, but it can only fulfill you to a point.

You'll feel unfulfilled if you're not expressing your light by creating things yourself. If you're not creating, you won't experience the Universe's unconditional love flowing through you and instead will only get tastes of it outside yourself.

If your only experience of love comes from others' work, it's easy to diminish your value. You may think other people are born with a natural gift to make fantastic art that touches people's hearts, but you're not.

Holding this belief puts that other person on a higher level than you, further reinforced by how your society values commercial success. If you compare yourself to others, you may gather evidence for a belief that says another person is better than you, but this belief is false.

Every person can channel the Universe's love through their creative acts. No person was born with a greater ability to do this than another. Although each expression of this love differs, everyone draws from the same source.

Some people's creative expressions give them what other people call natural talent. These people were likely encouraged to share their light at a young age, but that doesn't mean they have more light than you.

Everyone has an unlimited source of light, which is the Universe's love. So far, I've been referring to this light as each person's light only to make things easier to understand.

Each person's light refers to their ability to access the light within themselves, but the light you're channeling is the Universe's love. There is an infinite amount of this love available to everyone.

Each person doesn't have a pool of light that can be exhausted. Everyone connects to the same source. Some people have allowed themselves to express more of this light, but that doesn't mean they have more than anyone else.

Earlier on, we discussed how your ego is your set of conditioned responses that stop you from expressing your light. There is another side to your ego that we must discuss now.

Your ego can also take ownership of your light. When you express your light without acknowledging that it's the Universe's love you're channeling, your ego will think that the light is coming from itself.

When your ego takes credit for the light you express, it becomes more powerful because it believes it's generating all the newfound love you and the people around you are feeling.

It's essential to understand your source. The Universe is always your source and has infinite unconditional love to share with everyone. Nobody can ever own this love or have a greater right to it than anybody else.

Instead of seeing your ability to channel the Universe's love as your ego becoming enlightened, see it as your true self. Your ego is only a set of conditioned responses you've gathered throughout your life. To experience inner peace, you must let go of your ego.

No matter how much money, fame, or love you receive from others, it will never satisfy your ego because your ego is an illusion. Your ego has no foundation to stand on because it doesn't exist. It's just a set of conditioned responses with no tangible roots. To grow your ego is to increase your suffering.

Let go of this belief that you're the sum of your conditioned responses. Your true self is a vessel for the Universe's unconditional love. You're a channel, and the Universe's never-ending love enters your world through you.

The way you manifest and express this love is what makes you unique. When you let go of your ego and live from your heart, you experience satisfying peace and don't feel threatened by things outside yourself that seem to jeopardize your identity.

When you surrender your ego and express your light, nothing can bring you down or threaten your sense of safety. You see yourself as a divine child of the Universe, opening yourself to express its love. You also see all other humans as children of the Universe with the same ability to channel this love that you have.

Living from your heart inspires other people to do the same. Because there is infinite love available to everyone, there is no competition. Your highest potential is to take up as much space as your heart desires and shine your light fully. The beautiful design of your world is that every time you express your light, you add more love to the collective.

Everyone manifests the same love in their unique way. By being alive, you get the joy of experiencing the Universe's unconditional love through the art created by others in countless exciting forms.

Instead of being threatened or jealous of other people's light, see it as a gift. The light you see in others is the same light that lives in you. This light is the Universe's never-ending love for you that nourishes you and allows you to live a deeply fulfilling life.

ABOUT THE AUTHOR

Eric's journey started with a love for business as a kid that led him to live around the world, connecting with other like-minded people. After living in 8 countries, he had a sudden spiritual awakening during the middle of the night where he began channeling words such as, "wake up, it's all energy."

This spiritual awakening led Eric down a path of synchronicities where he completely gave up the business path and went all-in on his spiritual practices. After attending a never-ending list of spiritual classes from clairvoyant training, to breathwork, and crystal reiki meditation, Eric found his calling in the dance of life as an Author.

Now Eric spends his time writing books that empower you to reach your Soul's Highest Potential and has gained a large following on the social media apps TikTok & Instagram where he's sharing excerpts from his books.

STAY CONNECTED WITH THE AUTHOR

Visit the link below to find all of Eric's books & social media accounts:

www.ericjohncampbell.com

Printed in Great Britain
by Amazon

24774368R00037